Alexander Pope at Twickenham

Also by Alan Wall:

Poetry

Jacob
Chronicle
Lenses
Gilgamesh

Fiction

Curved Light
Bless the Thief
Silent Conversations
The Lightning Cage
The School of Night
Richard Dadd in Bedlam
China
Sylvie's Riddle

Non-fiction

Writing Fiction

Alexander Pope at Twickenham

ALAN WALL

Shearsman Books
Exeter

First published in the United Kingdom in 2008 by
Shearsman Books Ltd
58 Velwell Road
Exeter EX4 4LD

www.shearsman.com

ISBN 978-1-905700-99-8

Copyright © Alan Wall, 2008.

The right of Alan Wall to be identified as the author of this work has been asserted by him in accordance with the Copyrights, Designs and Patents Act of 1988. All rights reserved.

Acknowledgements

Some of these poems have appeared before in *Agenda*, *PN Review*, *Stand*, *The Spectator*, *BBC Wildlife Magazine*, *The Jewish Quarterly*, *Winnicott Studies*, *Outposts*.

Some have won prizes in the Cardiff International Poetry Competition, the BBC Wildlife Poet of the Year Competition and the Wells Literary Festival Poetry Competition.

The author is grateful to the Royal Literary Fund for two RLF Teaching Fellowships, one at Warwick University and the other at Liverpool John Moores. He would also like to acknowledge the AHRB/Arts Council Fellowship he was awarded in 2003, to work with the particle physicist Goronwy Tudor Jones.

Contents

Mandelstam in Exile 7
The Flash at Gresford 9

London
Thomas More in Chelsea 17
Alexander Pope at Twickenham 21
Samuel Johnson in Grub Street 25
John Soane at Lincoln's Inn Fields 26
Coleridge on Hampstead Heath 27
Coleridge in Highgate 28
John Keats at Wentworth Place 32
Richard Burton in His Marble Tent at Mortlake 33
Isaac Rosenberg in Whitechapel 35
Sigmund Freud in Hampstead 36
Ezra Pound at 10 Church Walk 37
Francis Bacon in Soho 38

Chronicle 41

The Flaying of Marsyas
The Flaying of Marsyas 65
Saint George in Retirement 71
Lot's Wife 75
A.L.F. 76
Ascetic 78
Hospital 79
John Milton at Bunhill 81

Lenses 83

Hearts to Keep This Law
Hearts to keep this Law 103
After Purgatorio Canto XVI 108
Shroud 112

To my Mother and Father

Mandelstam in Exile

It was a time of blizzards over transit camps
  When the age screwed tight its eyes
Raw from rubbing away the light. A time of
  Villages with disappearing names
Scattered like salt in the north. Wolf years
  Behind whose grin lay nothing
But the scorched earth of amnesia. A hunger
  Cold enough to eat the wind.
So this Dante once more paced the metre of his exile
  As Guelph and Ghibelline
Between them divided the days. In Voronezh
  His teeth crunched the bread's
Forgiving snow and, as the crust was torn,
  His emblematic tongue gave
Benediction. But night intruded and prevailed:
  A black hood gathered gently
Over the axeman's eyes. Night, that ransacked
  The apartment, turning up
Those beautiful equations discrediting paradise—
  Catalogued and packed away in boxes
They were shifted to the centre of the zone.
  There the temperature was zero,
The population nil, and famished verses drifted
  Over squares so dead
Euclid would have wept. There an iron lung
  Hushed with grey breath
The calendar's progress. A spider manoeuvred
  Round her frail necropolis.
Into the gauze mesh of her eye, stars disappeared
  As the weather told lies
To blindfold icons razored out of mute cathedrals.

Frosted acres out of which a spadeful of glistening
  Black earth protested.
A solid lake of milk on which a raven landed.
  Vladivostok. December. 1938.

The Flash at Gresford

To Goronwy Tudor Jones

In the Gresford Colliery disaster of September 1934, 266 miners lost their lives. Almost all the men's bodies were sealed into the pit and never recovered. At the subsequent inquiry no owner ever appeared. Half a century later a memorial was erected to the memory of these men. It is all that now remains of the Gresford Colliery.

The Flash is the name of the nearby lake, where miners would sometimes walk with their families.

1

A flash.
Past meets present
In an instant.
Each photograph halts time.
Faces are for ever thus.
There is no photograph of this.

Marshlight firedamp carburetted hydrogen methane,
A miner's litany of menace.
If aisles and alleys
Are not sprinkled with stonedust then coaldust
Ignites beyond any warning glow
Of Davy Lamp or Geordie Lamp
Ringing bells or running feet
The screams of men
Who know this final shift will not be ending.

Those the explosion doesn't take
Carbon monoxide does.
A cough into sleep
From which there is no awakening.

266 men.
September 1934.
Gresford Colliery.
Sealed in their underground seam.
The price of coal.

2

A Davy Lamp like a tamed owl
Hangs from a collier's hand
Wings retracted in metal sleekness
An Egyptian god surfacing from time's deposits
A falcon of industry
Eyes welded together into one steady glow.

When it jumps, jerks and brightens into blue.

A flash
(The Gresford flash)
The flash Sir Humphrey dreamed
His lamp might draw a line beneath
The living on one side
On the other, only black fossilised carbon.

One inquisitive atom
Spearing its beak into another –
That's all it takes –
Making 166 widows
229 orphans
One flat mining day in September.

3

Look around you, visitor;
Revenant from the curious future.
Not many have come back to see.
This is not Persephone's second home
The blazing halls of Dis
Through which a god strides, shouting orders.
Dirt corridors 2000 feet underground
Held up by crooked pit-props
Where a man must satisfy his needs
In sundry corners. The cage
Does not go up and down at your pleasure.

Matter simplifies itself at the first opportunity.
Bonding its atoms more tightly, then
Expressing the difference between first state
And second
As energy.
Gas, for example. Luminescent gas.

Such differences.

Women lay heads on pillows
As wives
To wake hours later as widows.

4

At the inquiry
Hartley Shawcross spoke for the owners
And took his fee.
Stafford Cripps waived his,
To speak for the miners.
None of the owners ever turned up.
Some men go down into darkness
So others might live in the light.
They worked for nine shillings a day.

Half a century later
The memorial
Made out of blue and grey slate
Welsh slate that's leached the mist from the air
As it does to this day in Blaenau Ffestiniog.
Perfect stone for rooftop and grave
The world's rain, it seems, already solid inside it.

(Always a curse to go down there
So said the myths
So many mouths
Full of earth
Eyes turning white with the darkness.
One thin seam is graveyard enough to swallow the sun.)

A pit wheel stands upright
As salvage from the enterprise
Stationary
As the others are now
And always, each day, flowers in vases.

No messages any more
Only fresh flowers in glassware.
Placed with such care
By fingers from somewhere.

5

Half a mile away is the Flash
A little lake
Pitmen would stroll around.

Why Flash?
'A pool, a marshy place,' the OED informs us,
Though in miners' usage there's always
Been the sense of a rapid subsidence
From workings underground
Like that other flash:
'A sudden outburst or issuing forth of flame or light';
And of a hydro-carbon: 'To give forth vapour at a temperature
At which it will ignite';
And lastly (the Dictionary speaks dispassionately):
'To scorch with a burst of hot vapour'.
Hard to read that without seeing faces.

266 faces.

The Flash is a great place for birds
Gulls black-backed and black-headed
In the briefest of migrations from the Dee.
Flutters of warm snow above glinting water.

Air feathers itself into brief commotions
Before they settle down again and the water
Rings them in widening circles.

The nearby fields afford such a variety.
Lapwings with their peewit treble
Tweezering the air.
Blue tits, robins, goldfinches,
Blackbirds, rooks and the occasional raptor.

How many colliers observed these birds each Sunday
Staring at the light all around them that would be gone again
Come Monday morning?

6

Two minutes walk away,
Wrexham and District Model Engineers Society
Steams up its painted miniatures.
The engineering skills
That built the mines and worked them once,
Scaled down now since the days of Brunel.

Boilers heat. Valved pressure hisses.
A whistle announces
One train ready at last for its tiny journey.

1

London

Thomas More in Chelsea

This gilded face looks out on the embankment, expressionless
  noting the sleeker bodies of the Japanese saloons —
My statue silts here at the margin of their progress.

Behind me the Old Church chapel where I knelt in prayer
  restored since the night in 1941 when four hundred
Bombers targeted London with pentecostal fire:

A thousand bodies counted, two thousand others wounded
  (what's my head weighed in gold compared to that
Or this mouse-whisper of my breath, these eyes long-blinded?)

Say that I'm made of bronze, of books and prayer-cards, a bust
  at the dingy end of red-brick sanctuaries
Paired up with Saint John Fisher, both veiled with dust

We thought we had escaped forever, bending to His will
  kneeling before the block and praying
Christ come quickly beneath the scaffolding on Tower Hill.

Thomas More, chancellor, author of *Utopia*, a laughter-driven
  tract Karl Kautsky recommended as part-Bolshevik.
A black feather on the frozen Thames, dropped by a raven.

Say I'm the prayer of everyone these last four centuries
  sent to me (care of heaven) from a thousand cells
Where men with steel smiles and syringes shoot disease

Into the veins of hope, say I'm nothing but an emblem
  faith calls to account, faith smiling before kings
For which each paternoster audit's richer than a dukedom.

Join me at the sharpening edge of the King's displeasure
   although our hospitality and table grow exiguous
And Alice mutters ceaselessly *Only a fool and his treasure*

Could separate so swiftly on a point of disputation —
   even Meg stares at me, wanly curious
To ponder the unaccountable extent of my misprision

For between the lion and his wrath's no place of peace,
   my prayers Saint Jerome answered with a smile:
The paw he pulled a thorn from bore no royal fringe of lace.

Henry's anger quells my lords, would indeed quell me
   did I not fear God's wrath a little more than his
(The judgement one of them bestows is final, gospels tell me.)

Yet now in this our time of tribulation I grow merry
   each meal a eucharist of bread, though seldom wine.
Son Roper's quit his heresy, confessing himself sorry

For the Lutheran rant I once found so tormenting,
   affairs of state slide off like golden chains
Since I have seen where Harry's heart is bending.

He'll have his new queen and he'll have a son
   if the cost is laying half the nation waste
Or taking an axe to necks he recently laid kisses on.

But English shires won't rouse from drizzled torpor
   though beckoned by the saints at lattices.
Anne gleams on in the frozen silver of her mirror.

Revelling, or ditched in sleep to quench his light
  outside his lawns are splashed with roses. Come dawn
you'll see the red ones blaze among the white.

Mistress Alice frets and swoops and claws away my plate
  her face pinched ferret-tightly as she goes.
Wooden plates, for cheese, dark bread and rabbit meat.

She liked it better when her mighty lord once held
  England's laws, a diamond turning on his finger.
For now her finery is pawned, her rooms grow cold

Whose fires have warmed ambassadors and poets, their wit
  fresh out of Europe might have skimmed her scalp
But she knew well enough the cost of entertaining it.

Once I laughed so loud against Erasmus whooping, Holbein
  dropped his brushes in the bowl and filled his glass.
He said to limn hyenas mating he might need more wine.

Now beneath the scalding acid of my wife's sharp tongue
  lurks the apothecary, fear. Praying out of earshot
She senses menace even in the shadows that I move among.

(And I'll have time there to repent the heart's diseases
  in the vermin cloister of a cell, before I'm put
Beneath the ancient haunting-ground of English mercies)

Why will you not bend, she says, *as have your elders?*
  Divines and scholars daily shift their ground
Remarking how their heads stand tickle on their shoulders

For Henry will never let me be, she understands.
  He doesn't want my silence but acclaim,
A kiss of absolution for the jewels on both hands.

But if my worldly prince assume such priestly graces
  then will he be lord of all that he surveys
Heaven and hell mapped out as royal hunting-places.

He'd have my mind. If that's impossible, then instead
  despite a love for me he pledged and once intended
He'll take, for his bleak consolation prize, my head

Together with whatever laws might query its removal. Now
  see Son Roper rush back breathless, close to tears.
The field that has lain fallow must receive the plough

To yield the hidden pearl that costs a man his kingdom.
  Officers from Lambeth moor their barge. On their return
They'd be obliged, they say, should I accompany them.

Alexander Pope at Twickenham

Swift is at sea already, returning to Ireland
   to raise his hyssop sponge
Into the face of that harried land

Leaving me here to my dwarf enclosure
   five acres of retirement
A buttonhole whose gap would disappear

Amid the uniform estates of Bathurst's Cirencester;
   a curiosity, a topographic fragment.
Here this last week Swift's de-commissioned jester

Traded rhymes with an unlicensed fool:
   now cloistered in the silence
I bend back to my cursive minuscule.

Twickenham: home to my softly-spoken house
   edged with a rainbow of flowers
And lifted lightly from Palladio's shadows.

(I could so easily have been that man
   whose lifetime's satisfaction
Was to engrave the apostles on a cherry stone

Or he who cut on two grains of wheat
   the Shema Israel
A liturgy entire for a mouse to eat.)

Trellised corners where a heart might soften
   see vines disintegrate
Slugs preponderate and spiders stiffen.

My feet move lightly as the blackbird's tread,
  I count how many heron nests
Have sunk their smashed eggs in the flood.

When Swift surveyed the inside of my grotto
  he proclaimed retirement in this life
Mere phantasy and monastic stillness ditto

Then back to the confinement of his deanery
  to stare at what his skull
Provides: the faecal daubs of prison scenery.

While the wind increases and the Muse of Smithfield sings
  let us consider eschatology
In contemplation of the four last things.

The earth could cough itself to death by drought
  (though surely not in England —
Each cloud's a reservoir to put the sunfire out.)

Raging atoms could blacken us with flame;
  the flood has visited before
And we are promised no two endings are the same

Promised not to die at least as we have died before—
  inquisitorial eyes that swam unblinking
Through silent palaces across the ocean floor.

Let it be ice—the burning ice. Unpunctuated winter
  with one pole planted firmly
In the liberties of parliamentary Westminster.

Imagine the prattle and the politicking silence
   hushed beneath one vast white
Cancellation of all eloquence within the Law's violence.

Newton's massive clockface of the skies
   eternity is counting on
Would gaze down on a world of creaking ice.

In Soho drinks already glaze their lips,
   liquor's crystal glass
Petrifying onto gothic fingertips

The Thames is mercury in a smoked phial
   clutching its discarded trolleys
And one blind doll smiling a septic smile.

On Hampstead Heath a fox's snout quivers
   at the vanished wind, alert
With fathoming bristles for what the chill delivers.

How still they lie under the frozen dome
   of Hampton Court, Chiswick and Kew
Fair nymphs still waiting for the last cab home.

Skyfulls of snow fetch fuller silences to come
   dropping a sheet of benedictions
Like altar linen over the alluvium of Twickenham.

Damp grass records the measure of my steps
   for a condemned man still must walk
To his last sacrament or first apocalypse.

Spine buckled, chest crushed, brain dry
   a meal warmed lightly over
Then fed rhyming to tubercle bacilli

More logical to cancel me inside the womb
   a dead letter dumped unread
Amid gifts rotting in the sack-cloth room.

Cousin Swift is away with the wound in his head
   to Dublin, intending no further trips:
I'll learn to read his passion with unmoving lips.

SAMUEL JOHNSON IN GRUB STREET

When I knocked Thomas Osborne to the floor
   for a gross impertinence imputing negligence
It was with the folio edition *Biblia Graeca Septuaginta*, 1594

A good book to lay a fellow flat with, sound and weighty
   in morals as well as pounds and ounces:
A clout for the rich insolence of the high and mighty.

John Soane at Lincoln's Inn Fields

We came upon them tracked through centuries with eyes
   that started shining in the the Italian sun,
Stones scorched Piranesi-black under the azure skies.

Wife to King Charles of Bourbon, Maria Amalia Christine
   had set her heart on digging up the past.
Now horses flanked in bronze and temple-gods are seen

In Neapolitan daylight blinking. The spinning planet
   turns down its massive cover to reveal
The ruin we retrieve out of the ruin heaped upon it.

(Imagine though how lapilli came hailing down the mountain
   till Vesuvius's lethal cough made lungs a prison
And one by one they fell like Tokyo commuters breathing sarin)

My classic sense I brought back home to London galleries
   granting a light I borrowed from serene antiquity
Applied in equal measure to mausoleums and distilleries,

All riddled with exotica. The sarcophagus from Seti's tomb
   lies in my crypt, though icons of mortality
Crowd convex mirrors in the empyrean of the Breakfast Room:

All the touring spirits my curators have manoeuvred
   now fly home to their comfort. Still outside
Lie homeless heads the earth itself will soon enough have covered.

Coleridge on Hampstead Heath

In Valletta honey-coloured softstone churches
   powdered the air at noon
While sun kissed flies and slept in ditches,

Gilded the sea's back, struck gold samphires into light.
   Angelus bells hammered the cracked sky
Startling a pair of dithering choughs to flight.

On Hampstead Heath today the world greens in its drizzle
   far from coral shipwrecks and the heat—
All horror left behind me with the vision's dazzle.

Now nearby they chase the dragon or sport needles
   (white powdersift in sachets)
Thus avoiding metaphysics, or Revelation's riddles.

If I had grown with them would headlights have found me
   in a tenement stairwell, tightening
The tourniquet while junkie faces mooned around me?

Coleridge in Highgate

On Hampstead Heath today I met John Keats, who bowed
gravely before me like Garrick bending to the crowd
though perhaps a mite more awkwardly

and for an hour or more we rambled:
I touched on nightingales, metaphysics,
mermaids, krakens, how premonitory ghosts resemble

wishes fashioned in the deep well of the mind,
what intricate veins connect our present
discomfiture backward through the wounds of time.

A pleasant fellow, a good listener
though he has I fear the pallor on him—
likelier to blaze briefly than glow dim.

I looked hard at his face once and I thought:
William, Dorothy, Nether Stowey's cottage, Alfoxden,
Ballads in the making, whole stanzas fought

over or deleted as the Quantocks flew.
The world resolved to making one line true
as cirrocumulus fled eastward from the Channel.

And now this pale young poet rides his steed
across the dream-transfigured heath
back to the chill bone cave inside his head.

Seeing such ravages as clearly as I do
explains in part at least how frequently I flee.
Thus at his age I became Silas Tomkyn Comberbache

(shifting my shapes like Vishnu) of the Fifteenth
Light Dragoons, to quit entanglement and debt.
Of the many I've gone to, that was the greatest length.

I saw myself in the cymbal-crash of battle
as steel shafts winced about me and the bugles trilled.
For two months I scoured filthy stables in the cold.

But Brother George pursued me with a stalker's concentration.
His grounds for my release — "INSANITY" — were accepted
with more alacrity than either of us expected.

I was enchanted by the sibilants in *Susquehannah*
and added two more with my *Pantisocracy,*
also engaged myself to marry Sara Fricker

though less to please myself than Southey,
who rightly wished decorum and propriety
to be, as we embarked for the Americas, our liturgy.

And then we didn't go. Instead Southey
calmly, slowly, responsibly, soberly,
suggested farm-work on a hill in Wales.

Somehow the noble notion of Pantisocracy
translated to such contiguous topography
seemed entirely ludicrous, even to me.

But marriage brought gentleness I'd not expected
as Sara cradled me to comfort in our cot.
Sorrows with their dull demeanours were deflected

then from Wedgwood a lifetime's annuity
made bread and board secure and buttressed thought.
Hazlitt hiked in homage all the way from Shrewsbury.

I set out journeying to map the modern mind
hearing, as I philosophised in Germany,
I'd lost one of the boys I left behind.

Poor Berkeley. Had I not strayed so far
he'd not have died, none ever can while I am near.
Love shifted from primary to secondary Sara

(In all the annals of those ancient heroes
was ever one who must contend
as I have done with these accruing Sara's?)

Friendship rotted, the Imagination slept,
out of the eyes of drowned men oceans wept.
This Singular-at-Sea was shipwrecked.

With laudanum the hours would gently melt
like butter on a griddle
an iceberg sinking through a sea of gilt.

I'd watch the candle's dancing blue and amber flame
Krishna's wheeling arms before Arjuna
whirring all creation's atoms, revealing the arcana

my mind has almost perished seeking.
The conqueror of sloth beheld Lord Brahma
enthroned upon the lotus and unspeaking.

Here the holy serpents made their sound,
their slithering and rattling a sanctus,
a chain that moors high heaven to the ground.

How merciless the symmetry that sees
us quell the wired veins of affliction
only by sharpening the needles of addiction.

That kind man Doctor Gillman's given me
his highest window to survey the town.
The city darkens every day that I look down.

From here in Highgate I can see the smoke of time,
its tainted breath coughed up into the sky.
I hear the bells of Ottery Saint Mary

fling the hour out with a jingled flurry.
On Hampstead Heath today I saw
a squirrel's spine snapped in the jaw

of a mongrel and thought of that Bacchic frenzy
men don feral masks for in Euripides.
No analgesic for this long disease.

Imagine all the same how stars might figure Paradise
each constellation tracing a pre-conscious state
I've hardly yet begun to theorise.

John Keats at Wentworth Place

Turning intelligence to soul requires a world of pain:
 heart's hornbook and the mind's bible.
Blood fades on an *ms*. A bibliographer remarks a claret stain.

Laying an ode out that a nightingale might fly across—
 Tom's cough irrupted through its metre:
A sweat-sieve of sheets records the retch of his distress

As Hampstead merely murmurs autumn, dabs a pastel blossom
 on its trellises. Bees dance coded intricacies
And oak roots inch through centuries to fathom

Leaf-rot growing mucus in a mole's tight tunnel.
 Above the blistered stucco of St John's
Two crows hunch up like pall-men at a funeral.

Richard Burton in His Marble Tent at Mortlake

One strong charge of electricity to the ulnar vein
   thus Isabel confirmed that I was dead
She closed my eyes and bound my jaw and then

Embalmers came and shot me full of fluids, relaying
   through my flesh a pallor of white marble.
Still I heard each word that they were saying

But fear itself had vanished. Soon disappearing too
   27 years of manuscript and notebooks
Burnt in that room by the woman I was married to.

My information failed to reach adventurers with razor smiles
   how to make a eunuch or ensure a maid
Remove the piquancy from urine, copulate with crocodiles.

She burnt the lot, my doughty and contractual protectress
   half a lifetime's work went in the holocaust.
Letters protested in *The Times*, but I couldn't have cared less

Even though my *Perfumed Garden* sent its fragrances to heaven.
   She was aware that out there scores of names
With scores to settle, swarm—vermin hungry to get even.

Then lovingly she laid me out in Mortlake in this marble tent
   under a nine-point gilded star
Where one Miss Goodrich Freer (of American descent)

Held seances inside the tomb for some months after
   I arrived in it. On their side came
No messages and on this only a little silent laughter

Though not as much as when I resurrected in a wax figure
   courtesy of that ghost warehouse, Madame Tussauds.
My wife dressed the anaemic mannikin in my clothes from Mecca.

Mortlake is unexciting, not unlike in some ways death itself.
   There comes a sudden bedouin disquiet
And I take my own *Arabian Nights* down from the shelf

To walk in grey disparity along the oar-flicked river
   Invisible to shouting flesh.
All translations like all men were made to live forever.

Once when I arrived at evening in some African kingdom
   (tiny, ramshackle, incompetent) the king had
A man crucified against the setting sun as fitting welcome.

Isaac Rosenberg in Whitechapel

You stare at us from photographs in the Whitechapel library
  stare into the erasure of your future
Like Klee's *Angelus Novus* blown into the catastrophe

Of history while gazing back at emblems time has traced
  (lineaments in stone, bronze, words)
And behind the melancholy charcoal shadows of your face

Already cannon-fire shrouds France and Flanders,
  already behind you silent synagogues
Weep sabbath flames and from the dead hearth, cinders

Are brushed and flicked into a blackened bucket:
  the library sign's been turned to "Closed",
Your name fades slowly somewhere on a reader's ticket.

Sigmund Freud in Hampstead

Godlike grown to self-forgiveness as the trauma sings
    where every secret trips itself and spills,
The tiniest vacuum forms a blister at the heart of things.

Vienna has chosen death, elected grey-beard Thanatos
    to rule the hearth of nimble Psyche.
Into her pale flesh he brands the geometric cross

And a radio enshrined beyond the lintel of each citizen
    wipes any film of contradiction from the scrolls.
History the tyrant's mistress, Clio the savage courtesan

Smiling her mirror smile. Out of the sun come runners
    dressed from the pages of a Greek mythology
Breathless with statistics under the fluent banners.

Ezra Pound at 10 Church Walk

What causes the ferocity and bad manners?
       EP, 1933

Clio's my muse, who's seen bad times of late.
   She owns a little river, trailed
By willows where English gentlemen have sat

Or waded through the current, casting on the water
   rainbows of feather, heaving home a creel
Spilt with the splendours of already-tarnished silver.

A dispute arose among her children late last year
   leaving the family fractured in dissent.
All talk's of coin, yield, mortgages, where Waller

Laid a song that Henry Lawes choired into voices.
   A fraction of the issue she has spawned
Forms now an errant crew and as the beloved faces

Stare from wasting trellises, these row hard upstream
   away from her untended moorings.
Poison's stealing half the water's life, the family name

No longer prompts a smiling handshake in the City;
   the little ivy-veined hotel
Bought-out to give ground to a concrete factory.

Dead fish, luminescent sewage, and one night a corpse.
   Though her mouth moves still, words turn
Back inside her throat and only dribble leaves her lips.

Some weekend soon we'll leave the traffic here behind
    (the lethal tongues, the babel of dispute):
I'll square up to those boys, face to face and mind to mind.

Let's pray, remembering that lady's beauty and her courage
    I recall the love she felt at first for all of them
So keep my fists and language poised, and not grow savage.

Francis Bacon in Soho

To the east the manor of the Krays, the Ripper and Dan Leno
  to the west the dark and paint-besmirched atelier —
These two hands are the annihilated clock of your casino.

Needlemen and rentboys throng the streets
  offering ancient solace. You wake
Booze-bleary in the dawn upon a cumulus of sheets

To hear a pope in the ghost-geometry of his baldachino
  scream as loud as any debtor of the Krays
Or laughter-clenched heads in the vaudeville dark of Dan Leno.

2

Chronicle

to P. J. Kavanagh

1

We start from the granite building, Westquay House

The estuary swells and sinks beneath us
Raising and dropping the clinkered boats riding at anchor
Each with a sentinel perched on its rim
Where the crafting of man meets the weather, sky turns
Mirror and light is reversed.

A kittiwake swerves upward over and over to
Stalling-point, then dips into graceful decline:
A descant on the odds against itself.

The tide here has ghosts on its back.
They draw its silk sheet off to the Atlantic
A grey film punctured by scurried winds.

Dun and grey sandstone and shillet
And out of the far-fetched water
A ridge of rolled stones the sea spat out
Round-shouldered, with the odd vein of quartz
That loops a ragged equator around them.

When the tide relents
Bars breach the ebb into islands
Prints washing foetal up through the river's fix.
Each day, low jets from RAF Chivenor
Circle like mating gulls
To simulate the heart's thunder
Their fledglings terror.

Oystercatchers stalk the salt's edge.
Low cloud is dragging the hills, leaving

A vague smear of drizzle.
A car coughs into life.

On the rusted Russian fishing boat a sailor
Swings up his face to the sky
Aspersed with rain for his journey.

The fridge behind me lengthily shudders.
I monitor the thrumming in its heart.

2

So scatter a handful of years and watch
That huge wall battered down, stones
Tumbling to one side or another.

We have crouched before plastic boxes
Following this. By the time
Our fisherman is home again
No longer does the peaked stone cap
Intrude upon a re-named square.

And from the east the soldiers say
More soldiers marched out of an endless winter
Back-lit and numinous
Boots worn out, their bellies
Whispering a memory of food.

Liberation's ardours.

Our own came back
Leaving their Tipperaries and their guns behind
To a land the future would deliver.

3

Watch terraces collapse.
Hear masonry's soft thud
As plaster leers from gashes
In the wallpaper.

For now joy's fled these windows.
At night the spiders take their quarry
Undisturbed. Rats no longer move so tenderly.

The final guests arrive
Wheeling their fanfare of banality:
Rubber, diesel fumes and steel.

Why rummage through the rubble
For their tokens?

Already they are far away and re-located
With hardly a lament for streets they exited.

They've shifted to
A modern up-to-date development.
High rise.
Miles of it to stare across.

4

Pugin's dream was different. Spires
That trained themselves on heaven
A skyline cluttered only with belief.

Blessings slanting on rain-softened shores
Craftsmen, plainchant, handworn chisels
Bells summoning monastic choirs

Each stony De Profundis sounding the horizon.
But the bull wheezing in the nation's frost
Snorted pressurised steam from steel nostrils.

5

Top valves blew and wept over the boiler lagging.
Juggling eccentrics the engineer coaxed
Drive wheels to reverse. One thick white blast then
Showers of gold as steel over iron
Whined to a halt.

The coal came from a good thick seam.
Swarms of pitmen crawled through veins
To haul it up. The cage spilled out
A proper tribe of Africans
At the end of every shift.

Should industry occlude the sun
Still the sky was ample. Every Sabbath
See the grand dispersal: machines at rest
Heavens zeroing to blue.

Down where the river slowed in its gleet
We raised a house of worship, ample enough
For most of our workforce.
All in the purest of Greek styles.
Its Doric portico darkens already
With the engines' breath.

6

To the revolutionary doctor in the British Museum
The limp embroidered shapes present themselves
Like visiting cards embossed with gold.

He swiftly diagnoses clutter in the soft room –
The contemporary owner's need to press his shape
On everything his body touches.

Observe the London residences of the masters.
How furniture sits dreaming of them all day long
While polished blades employ a surfeit of mirrors.

Spruce, lacquered, buttoned-up, they see their form
Paid back to them in courtesies of plate glass,
Glinting counters, the decanter's prismed edge.

These rooms they so made theirs provide no exits now.
To curtain off the servile forms and prim resemblances
They have to make arrangements in hotel rooms

A stone's throw from the mainline station
And only two hours ride out of Victoria.
There a certain Mrs Jones who travelled independently

Reading alone in a separate closed compartment
Can join you at your leisure in a double with a view.
There the ribbons fall, the stays unfasten

Stockinged legs are peeled while gauze
Frisks gently back and forth across the window
Catching a light breeze off the sea.

There at a price they might be seen
As they were not before, these gentlemen.
Touched unexpectedly as if the skin were new

And lived in silent protest at starched linen
Razored cheeks and creaking leather
Dark coverings of serge and worsted.

Afterwards he'll smoke a small cigar
Discreetly check his watch
Then as he makes his way

Through those familiar streets he'll maybe
Murmur to himself how odd it is
Possession and desire fall out so quickly.

7

Scatter another handful of years
Here at the shore where scorched blades
Are dumped amongst bones in the stormwood.

From under the water
Drowned whispers turn back the tides.
From darkening headlands goat eyes watch
Waves break in the salt diaspora and vanish.

This is our island
Perched at the ocean's edge
Precarious.
When the weather starts time stops
Time brought here by mainland men
Who bore aloft chrome hoops like gleaming monstrances
Effigies the sun might burn their hands with.
Then sped back to the shining windows of metropolis.

Here the ancient music, finding a mountain
Persists still in its delicate lament.
The shapes they sought passed through their lenses
Unhalted in the lightless room.
Those creatures live on air so thin
The birds fall through it.

When we cut into the earth
For something to give flame to
Out pour arrowheads and jewelled torcs
Worked loose now from the flesh they nuzzled.
The children of those warriors set sail
Searching for a continent of slaves and gold.

When they return one day
Their eyes – bright, unaccountable –
Will light on their women's bodies like strangers.

Our towers in any case were long ago ruined.
Our defences handed over to the sea.

On the bluntest cliff this coast affords
A grand oaken cross
Bids the Atlantic breakers cease.

In the weathering hulks of our chapels
Beneath a pair of soft hands raising
The benediction of the disc
We pray the old gods have departed.

And if not departed, not angry at least.

8

So much silence lies in smashed stone tracery.
The chantry's requiem of tongues is gone
Crumbling to dust in shallowing inscriptions.

Defeated heraldry on battered tombs,
Aves, paternosters and the murmured beads.
Ghosts in ragged cowls through ruined chapels

Shuffle as the wind snaps leaves
Against the altar's lichen-stone.
Rood screens hammered down for timber.

The bright new world of learning
Burns so many shadows off, it leaves
A man missing half what walks behind him.

An antiquary sends us
Postcards from the gloom:

Wine stains still visible
On the Irish chalice's chased silver
I scooped out from a bog one damp sojourn.
Its consecrations done, it stands beside
A senatorial bust, the marble veined,
Eyes riddled with a vacancy
The years to come will bring.

One smoked phial encloses a bat's foetus
Bobbinned round by witch's hair
The victim drowned during the Wiltshire trials
Early 20's I'd say, raven-coloured
Still matted from her dousing.

And just last month in Bermondsey
I came across a small miscellany of verse
Predominantly Latin, bound in vellum
Warping already with humidity
(Thus I suppose the unborn deer continues breathing).
It's snug amongst the incunabula
In diverse tongues I've gathered here –
One's scatological: rantings against
God, the flesh and women.
A driven monk most likely
Itching with lust on some stony monastic outcrop.

In with the scatterings, a meteor fragment
Found by a shepherd one December morning
Speared into a scarp near Richmond, Yorkshire.
Cost me a florin to prize it out of Mr Jeremiah Higgs
Who claimed a single touch of it
Could cure the scrofula.

Above my desk, exquisite though stained,
Hermetic fragments from the Spanish exile
In Hebrew script, begin:

'What sparks inhabit wayward man and what
Fine dust will lift, what eyes rinse clear
When the ruins of those generations gone before
Awake out of their melancholy to enchantment?'

Tempera flakes off as the oakwood buckles
But the eyes of the icon
(Byzantine, Crete, circa 550)
Still stare out from the ruins
Of their painted world, unblurred.

9

Freeze that frame, then point the lens towards
Museum shelves. One holds a jewelled hilt:
Sole remnant of the battle
They sing about still
Where half a tribe went down
To prove allegiance. Its blade
Sunk in the mud somewhere, despatched
A throng of souls to mute stone gods.

That fragment of the true cross
Is a Palestine cedar
The years have mottled down to ochre.
And the blade in the corner was
Fired and hammered in Clerkenwell
Engraved with the device
      ANNO DOMINI 1071
Not damascened, but plain and purposeful.

All of these things had their uses.

10

Lord of this land sir
Frosty acres;
Sixty winters

Creased each hill
Into my memory.
What my hands pull

From yielding earth
My father's rooted there
Crooked with toil.

That clinkered barn
Slant on the valley's rift
Outlived his storms

As she has mine.
So will this wall
I built

Outlast my sons and theirs
Till one, warming
Inside to other men's fires

Sleeps as night wind
Slaps down to the nondescript scrub
One stone after another.

11

From here you see the oilships steam to shore,
Helicopters clatter out towards the rigs
Next month's workers wombed inside them.

Northeasterlies provide bleak music
Ancient spaces caught between each blast.
Foxes in holes, deer on the hills,

Snow plays host, laying its lace coverlet
To the salt's edge. The celebration's started.
Only our children couldn't come – so faraway

The city, blinking vast forgetful lights.
Their bright faces, cooling, distant,
Are stars once counted through a broken window.

12

Framed photographs fade imperceptibly
Beneath the weight of eyes.

Even the long skirts that bloomed into orchids
In Bert Hardy's Brownie along the Blackpool promenade
Are gone, and the mill-girls' laughter gone with them.
Ribbons of proprietorial smoke
Ungather like braids from terracotta chimneys.

And if the tanker freighted with crude
Is smashed by the waves, already beneath it
Dolphin shark and whale comprise
Anthologies of salt slaughter.

How easily the nib weeps ink.
How swiftly lists turn into litanies.
Fossils at peace in the chalk
Await the tick of the geologist's hammer.

Above you a gull's white line
Demolishes perspective
Its arcs across receding skies
Outcompassing report.

Instruments shine happily: they do their duty.
Dictaphones click off through city offices.
Faxed bulletins are laid to rest
In dust-free files. Tomorrow
They'll wake us to tonight's disasters.

Already, corridors of deep pile carpet
Quench your sound. Your clothes

Dipped surreptitiously in paper bags
Are spirited away by the smiling porter.
Inside this tower, time is yours
Measured out by digital displays.
The lines connect and your voice carries
From L.A. to Geneva
From Auckland to the Finnish coast.

Out there those sparefleshed northern warriors
Whose prows intoned the sea's language
Were salted to composure once.

The riverlights are drenched with smoke.
The white discs of their faces
Slide into the future and become occult.
Crocus births in snow.

If you disconnect your terminal
You can hear the same winds:

13

Imagine first: on a sea-slammed outcrop of dead volcano
A walrus is drying his tusks, sated with clams
In blear December sun.
                        Inland a fraction, lost
From battle, a footsoldier bent double in mist
Sings softly to himself a Latin canticle.
Requiescat scrapes point over parchment.
The chronicle accrues; a warm wax dribble of cloudy tears
Thickens the candle as this parchment fills.

Imagine then: 2 boats, long, swoop-prowed
Rolling the silk-glide swell
Oars working like the legs of a clumsy insect.
What visitors are these for whom cold villages
Ignite upon arrival?

A monk in the scriptorium is conjuring smoke
From the gospelled words of his redeemer.
A demon spits fire through the margin. His mind
Meanders back to years when Arthur reigned
And forward to the days when navigators
Will loop out like ecliptics from Gravesend
Searching for fresh lands where each mole burrow's
Precious with silver
Rabbit holes lumbered with gold.

14

Sail turns to steam turns to oil
And forests erode, hillsides hacked out and scorched
Till valleys vein with railway and roadway,
Viaducts pacing the fells.

A time and a half of the circling gull. Now imagine:
A sky crammed with metal, buzzing like clumsy insects,
Props thrashing the air. Come to drop fire
Onto cities. Over dereliction and the dusty flesh
Sirens are wailing.

Lastly imagine peace: the headland forbidden
Tricked out in warnings and wire
And abandoned to the army as a tribute of war.

A dead battery, standard ordnance issue,
Leaks its secrets into the poisoned soil:

An eyedrop of rusted water
Every second month.

20 yards away, the sea.

Coda

Cactus and fern,
Green for the many.
Work hard, you'll turn
Small coins, mint money.

Tenement, field,
They reach for each other.
Suburbs unfold
As meadows ungather.

Inhabit them. Rain
Rinses your cars.
Soft tyres spin
On the earth's hard floors.

In time you'll return,
Since old fuels drive us.
Study fern or some other green
Unflowered survivors.

3

The Flaying of Marsyas

The Flaying of Marsyas
(i.m. R.B. Kitaj 1932–2007)

A chicken's skin being no use
To man or beast
Unlike its liver and breast

Which provide paté
And the clammy strips added
To a high-class Caesar Salad

They die shrivelled but intact—
Our often flu-infected poultry
Whom we murder first and then dissect.

Unlike me. A satyr
Hairy then, half-goat
Providing Morocco bindings for your classic volumes,

Where one may philosophize
Over the removal of a beast's raw skin
Which any competent god can supervise.

But Apollo was more than competent:
A torturer of some finesse,
This beardless worshipper of his own intent.

His smooth-skinned life-assessing smile
Echoes even here in the gloomy
Steerage cabins of the Underworld.

I still see his finger uncurl
Like Oedipus before the Sphinx
Or a lordly toper signalling midnight drinks;

And what his index finger indicated
Was the precise rate at which
My epidermis should be decorticated.

Down here I walk around
Carrying my own carcass
Like a gunny bag.

My howl's intact
A sort of skinny gargoyle,
A Veronica's napkin of mute, flayed fact.

Michaelangelo has St Bartholomew
Doing the same thing
On the Sistine Chapel ceiling.

The saint looks more horrified than I do,
But then the centuries have lessened
To some degree my initial feeling

(rage, incomprehension, self-pity,
heart pounding, head reeling,
as inch by inch my hide came off).

And after they flayed Bartholomew
They crucified him. There's pain.
Belt and braces, then belt once again.

Never as popular as crucifixion
The most practical annihilation
Requiring only rudimentary carpentry

And three old nails, flaying
Needed specialists, as your plastic
Surgery does now. Cosmesis

I believe you call it. A lengthy business.
What they did to me took a lot
Longer than what they did to Jesus,

Calling for patient craftsmen while it lasted,
This archaeology of the body—
But still its devotees studied, improved, persisted.

If it's only fur you're after, call it skinning,
Though unless the animal is actually dead
This is terminological fine-tuning –

I'm half-animal and I know.
Amerindians flayed only the scalp
Thereby preventing entry to post-mortem hunting.

Assyrians flayed any captured whelp
Then nailed his skin to city walls
So future loyalties should not be wanting.

The Aztecs regarded it as one more
Colourful aspect of their sacrifices.
Medieval Europe carried on designing blades

Razors, various multiple devices,
Swiss Army knives devised by Bosch.
The Chinese were still at it in 1905,

A thousand cuts needed there
While the haemorrhaging victim stayed alive
To complete the ritual perfection.

In the Talmud Rabbi Akiva who taught Torah
Was for his pains flayed by the Romans
Hardly a mile from the agora.

Pagans, Christians, Jews:
There's no sectarian need to choose:
Torturers, you see, are mostly ecumenical.

Uses? Is there a practical side
To this age-old activity,
A useable hide?

After flaying, the Emperor Valerian
Was turned into a footstool.
And in Billy Wilder's 1945

Documentary, in the commandant's office
At Buchenwald, lampshades were said to be made
Of the tattooed skin of inmates, dead or alive.

There is then, as you can see, a wealth of data
In our underground library and cinema
And plenty of time to research the matter.

Once dead we quit all feeding
On anything but ghosts and shadows
So – a virtual eternity for study and reading.

Nietzsche I reckon had a point:
The Apollonian and Dionysian
Are at war as long as god meets man –

Or goat, since I am half and half.
Suffering itself can never be conveyed. Titian in 1575
Comes as close as anyone can.

The agents work away, my brothers weep.
The flesh comes off inch by inch.
Incisions shallow, agony deep.

Swift: 'Last week I saw a woman flay'd
And you will hardly believe how much
It alter'd her person for the worse.'

I'll believe it, Jonathan. No difficulty.
Forgive my knife-edge precision
But what you meant here, I think, was flagellation,

To which the flaying aspect
Is incidental, if far from pleasant
For a lustful, fleshy, blood-filled Irish peasant.

She lived to tell the tale though.
I didn't. I arrived down here,
Dedicated to the hatred of Apollo

Which god of light and reason I detest.
Who insisted the notes from his lyre
Were indisputably, insuperably the best.

God of certainty and calculation.
I found a flute a goddess had discarded
And played it till the creatures of my nation

Climbed from their trees and trembled.
Messengers flew down from the sky,
The seasons were reversed and humbled.

I'm as good as you, Lord, I said
To the mighty god Apollo.
Now he still rules and I am dead.

And the worst thing of all
In this Piranesi prison of his?
Each day I must listen to his harmonies

Which are broadcast from dawn until midnight
Between here and the first star's fire.
All you ever hear is his lyre.

Saint George in Retirement

I've made this cave my hideaway
Far enough outside the city walls so I can't hear
That wretched mayor announce himself each market day.

His daughter thrives, they say. No thanks to him
Who sent her with a number round her neck out through
These killing-fields. I only saved her in the nick of time.

Later her virginity was offered up but I declined.
Take a look at Donatello's cast of me,
You'll see I'm sealed within the shield I stand behind—

It's pedestalled over in the corner there, beside
The spear (admittedly a little rusty)
I plunged into the creature's leprous hide.

My glory-days for sure, providing copy non-stop
For each late edition of the Chronicle.
(If I fidget in this chair, that's my gyppy hip.)

I'd offer you some sherry but the cleaner's swigged the lot.
A phial of dragon-blood's left over,
They say it's honeying as dittany but it's past its date

As I am frankly, ending my days out here
Listening for that mayor's piggish squeal,
Giving interviews in which my age-old prejudices flare.

To business: My mother spent her hours before the screen
Mourning each grainy film, all the historic re-runs:
Shallow graves, mute shadows, Jack Kennedy's assassination

As she scooped pills out of a commemorative amphora
And washed them down with gin and tears.
A son's mother is *per se* a goddess so he must adore her

At least until the milk stops flowing, but you'll understand
As soon as Diocletian's circus tent-flaps opened
I left mother to her griefs. For me, the Holy Land,

Sacred footsteps, magma cooling the skin of Zion.
Let's see now, what do I remember?
A shepherd's limbs nosed by his sheep, lion-

Stink still on him. War-zones. Checkpoints. Mangled sidings.
Supermarkets rubbled by concealed devices.
Rumours of guns in empty tenements, sociology's sad tidings

And a clutch of students once, on a boat in the Aegean,
Reckless with intelligence and unpatrolled beliefs.
One was Antigone whispering lethally of Creon.

She opened and then stitched me up again
Her crimson-welcome a bird's silk flutter,
Love's blood-rich purse under the Patmos moon.

I bought a horse at landfall, never looked back
Though hearing still the secret language of her body
Chanting cabbalas of whispers on the varnished deck.

I found that village where they chased the dragon's tail
In dirty corners, their wages blown on memory's extinction
As one by one their children stepped in frail

Meanders out to meet the monster's hunger.
Mister Mayor was explaining to a crowded church-hall how
A virgin's life might expiate the dragon's anger

And while he spoke, his medals clanged their fear.
Visored I set out at dawn and found her chained.
My horse, catching the air's black madness, began to rear

Steam, stagger. Whinnies met my spurs as I
Wheeled round to find it crouching there
High on the rock. All I could see was one vast eye

Ringed red like the inferno, sooty spittle
Of impossible desire puckering its socket,
A scaled gut decorated with trophies of charred dottle.

Breath of an oven belching flame, urine, meths
Breath like wine after a lifetime's souring
Breath like the calculated smell of numbered deaths

As my spear sprang to life, a caduceus
Writhing charmed serpents down the dragon's
Throat, releasing small ghost-voices: "O Sir, don't slay us

And we'll remain your faithful captives all our lives."
I smelled the chew and slobber as they smoked
Through his intestines. Spear, sword, knives,

All busy with death's surgery, tattooing
The beast's number onto the beast's slack brow.
My mind could barely follow what my hands were doing.

Then I unclasped the young girl from her post and bid her
Take her wound back home until its proper season.
Last year a widowed merchant probed the cave inside her –

It's warmer than this one, I hope. Perhaps
We could stop now till tomorrow for I really must lie down.
This damp's no help; when it rains the ceiling drips

But you'll be used to rain, coming from England.
I was honoured when you made me patron saint,
I hear my ensign red-and-white's much in demand.

That sketch you're pointing to, I'm proud of it:
Exactly the way he flamed and quivered as I sank the spear.
A formidable opponent, no doubt of that.

Despite this body-rot, my memories have not diminished.
Tell me again the title of your thesis;
Promise you'll send a photocopy when it's finished.

Take the record with you; I'm afraid it's scratched.
If you're staying at the George, avoid that mayor –
He trawls the archives, getting his photographs retouched.

Lot's Wife

One salt tear is ocean enough
to swallow the earth and stars.
I stand here as my husband shakes me
furiously shakes me
and the snow and the ash fall about me
in the smooth glassy winter
of my world.

A.L.F.

Celery, carrots, potatoes and bread
don't bleed, don't get dragged from their cribs
before dawn, or stacked into lorries
knee-deep in blood-spattered straw...

Thus the shape of Cain's sacrifice
spelt out in rising smoke
haltingly, the right words
not easy to form
beneath his smouldering prayer-shawl.

He reasoned it thus:
Would you eat anything?
Swallow nightingale live
for its warm liquid song
catch the pulse of it swelling?

And if not then why not?
Do you imagine a cow
is any less kind than a songbird?

Abel's offering we know the Lord accepted
Cain's He returned:
In one brother's palm suddenly
a stone flourished
and the breeze inscribing Abel's brow
found a rubric, purple and crimson
for its text.

When the Lord at last came back
He whispered underneath the wind
where Cain was cooling his grievance:

Your brother. Can your mouth form
Whys and Wherefores
in that wilderness of explanation
your parents have chosen for home?

Cain smelt the blood on his finger
swung up his face to heaven and answered:

I only did to him
what I watched him do to them
that carnivore, eating the faces you fashioned.
He was himself stained badly inside by slaughter
like the smoke in an oven
like black smoke stains and scratches
inside a huge municipal over-used oven.

Ascetic

Perfected my withdrawal
somewhere around the seventh month

commenced oblique analysis
of those who visit supermarkets

hang washing out
have babies, otherwise

keep turning the old world
round its axis

feeling myself I'd strayed
far into the tangle of a foreign language

minus grammar and vocabulary
but listening intently

as some starved beast against the wind
catching promises of hunger and satiety

claw rump and febrile flesh
up there just out of sight

scratching hard earth
thawing out the winter in its heart.

Hospital

Unrol a lawn from your imagination
People it with figures robed in white
Like the chosen in the Book of Revelation

But these don't sing, their eyes aren't bright
Or if lit up at all it is with terror,
Casualties of shell-shock or gas-inhalation.

Where London marries well and enters Surrey
Picture the lime-washed Doric portico
Built for the first earl. *A grateful nation*

Wishes to express, etceterah etceterah.
Causing too much trouble with his version
Of battles misconceived, good men squandered —

Pension him off and caulk his blather, ration
His speeches, have his pamphlets laundered.
Requisitioned during the Great War

Its acres of retirement deemed a perfect foil
For the disintegrating wits of neurasthenics
To be re-assembled and made whole.

A tradition started by a staff sister
Who lost a husband and a brother at the Somme
Leaves a shilling oxidising on the windowsill

Of every trooper. To punctuate the mayhem
And the murmuring they're billeted among
Her voice trills out each day, announcing

When you are well enough to take that coin
And spend it, we'll bid you and your charts farewell.
Through the night the darkness crushes in

Oozing its flummery and jabber, for all
The world like Flanders mud. Scrubbed pink fingers
Bear aloft a tray of glittering needles

Each dawn to drain the trenchland of its riddles
Its air of insect sickness where the vermin
Rot. On every disinfected sill

Rust obliterates each day
The King's profile on the coins of servicemen
Who stare at windows bleared with rain

Or shattered into starbursts by the sun;
Who listen intently as beasts might listen
On this ward even as nothing gets spoken.

John Milton at Bunhill

1

Approach him, stone eyes glazed under a vitreous sky:
The blind maintain a wary welcome.
The house that survived the Great Fire is now gone
Though his shade stands secure. Motors blur by,
Occupants tuned to the radio's lilt and drone
Speeding hither and thus through the kingdom.

2

Approach him as he edges towards Bunhill Fields
(Ancient haunting-ground of English mercies)
Where Blake, Bunyan and Defoe lay still
In the plotted posthumous lives one grey meadow yields.
The bones of these sundry masters of dissent
Settled at last and held to their covenant.

3

What would our Puritan scrivener have made of Blake
Who died without a flicker, serenely singing?
His verse twins them both on one antinomian track,
A depth-charge electric with sexual longing,
A salmon-run, a rainbow-flash of contrariety,
Reading *Paradise Lost* with Catherine, nakedly receiving society.

4

Milton turns in the traffic, he has nothing to hide,
Ghost-days no longer bitterly married.
England spurned the new year's bride
For rotting shrouds and a body long-buried.
His flesh like the Nazarite's flesh had been chosen—
All flesh is grass that's not yet risen.

5

Regicide penman the axe passes over—a power-line
Crackles and spits in the liberal rain.
You hear spirits of heaven encrypted, Satan
Hurled headlong from heaven's throne once again:
Godless critics lament how in telling your story
You covered one hellish rebel with incandescent glory.

6

Swiftly down Bunhill Row, then west to the Church
Of St Giles Cripplegate, or what's left of its stones
After the bombs that fell amid falling flares.
Not that this final blitzkrieg unsettled you much:
Georgian louts had long before dug out your bones
Selling them to casual passers-by as souvenirs.

4

Lenses

to Bernard Sharratt

1

Alexander Topcliffe owned this house
built the small observatory in the garden
from whose stone shell his telescope
often protruded at midnight
to peep at constellations,
its polished brass glinting
like a conger's flank.

In his study, shining grimly,
a microscope through which he scrutinised
blood pricked from his finger
the ghost-dance of his own disease.

Flasks and retorts in his cellar
chortled as the compounds intermarried.
Above, an astral sphere
held scatterings of stars so he might
track the shifting heavens.

On his table, he played the planets
round and round
about themselves, his index finger
standing in for *Primum Mobile.*

2

To calculate the moon's year
or spectrum colours from white light
a man should retire
from the satirical city
live in social darkness
while meteors flare

reputations grinding the lenses
of their own enlargement

Should remind himself
as Alexander Topcliffe did
all other metals are unripe gold

So let the leaden-footed
or mercurial
pursue their strategies

Live alone
in a cold corner of your field
bless the winter

3

Topcliffe bowed his head
as Restoration buried Commonwealth.
Exhausted with turmoil
he had no appetite as Milton did
to blaze on grandly in the dark.

In any case the dark inside his blood
was eating him.
He studied this
with bemused precision
as he counted stars.
Kept diaries of his own extinction.

The field he boasted too severe
to facilitate the carriage of a gentleman
fills now with the film-crew's cars.

4

The man's a knot of contradictions, which is what attracted me to the subject: a man of science fascinated by the Kabbalah, a member of the Royal Society who spends half his days pondering Revelation, an astronomer at the forefront of the thought of his day who believed in alchemy, a contemporary of Isaac Newton and Christopher Wren who was once an officer in the New Model Army, but accepts the return of King Charles the Second on his return from the continent. A man revered among the brightest scientific minds of his day retiring here to one of the remoter parts of England on the North Yorkshire coast. "To enter my darkness" he said. "The stars shine brightest in the dark."

Became a recluse, keeping these diaries in which we can feel the actual pulse of his time; in which he watches his hope for the republic die, then watches himself die too, from a rare blood condition the science of his day had no name for.

What's most moving to me, despite all the pain and uncertainty, is his faith in the life of the mind—a belief he never relinquished.

5

This is Whitby, which once had a thriving whaling fleet. Here James Cook learned his famous seamanship, serving on the plying colliers. The ruins on the hilltop represent what's left of the Abbey where in 664 the Synod of Whitby decided the fate of the English Church. These ruins provided the eerie background for Bram Stoker's *Dracula*. A few miles back from the coast stands Ingleton Hall, originally a Tudor farmhouse, where Alexander Topcliffe spent the last eight years of his life.

6

The camera jackdaws down upon the Abbey
scans the pantile roofs of Whitby
hops the hills until it comes to
Ingleton Hall.

    Round and round
the helicopter circles, a zoom lens
prying more intently with each loop
that hybrid northern building, its tiny
Jacobean porch, the sandstone
black now from rebuffing
the northeasterlies, the little
unglazed loggia, fields of rough
grass all about it, then off
suddenly on an eagle's soar.

7

Why look so long at stars?
A man could find his peace among the distant dead
calculating revolutions, fathoming ellipses
from the light that scatters
through murky waste.

                        Sometimes
pressing my eye against the lens
I can forget in their indifferent movements
the motions that quicken
in my own slowed blood
those whispered microscopic meals
quenching hermetic hungers.

8

The telescope is now screwed firmly into the eye of Galileo. I move around the sun, he said. He might have lowered his voice a little, indeed fallen silent, but a whisper resounded through the centuries with more clarity than the pilgrims' cries of his day.

Topcliffe too had a reflecting telescope, mounted on a cup and ball joint, and focused by a screw — similar to Newton's though considerably larger.

His nocturnal activities might have made him suspect in a town, for superstition is the obverse everywhere of human thought, but placed here a mile or so on the hills above Whitby, his investigations were likely to disturb nothing but the owls and bats.

9

Woken at dawn
by the woodpecker's impertinence,
a rainbow-flash of green and red
scrabbling the hollow cedar.

Clouds power inland.
Sky shifts
its moisture about.
(The kittiwake's speed
a visible sign
of the wind's strength).
My one hawthorn, a windvane
rusted on its axle
points always south-westerly.

The pain increases.
It intrigues more and more
how the conscious mind
registering, indeed enduring
pain, yet distances the same phenomenon
for analysis and contemplation.

The pressure of discomfort
on the mind's manoeuvres
might explain in part
the imagination, its excesses.

The Royal Society still frets at
metaphor, that inexact
disturbance of our thought.

10

Lady Talgarth to Alexander Topcliffe

Sir,

I begin to understand your long preoccupation.

Now I see what you mean by being given new vision. How before Galileo no human eye had ever seen the satellites of Jupiter, no hand ever drawn up a map of the moon, its craters and shadows.

Perhaps at times the rough-cast features of the moon remind you of my own poxed face?

And perhaps you prefer to keep us both at a like distance?

You never pressed your body on me
when we were left alone
for hours at a time
but observed always
        a stellar propriety.

11

It seems certain that Lady Amanda Talgarth loved Topcliffe, but whether he ever loved her is harder to fathom. Her correspondence is unmistakeable in devotion; his own in return seems, at the first opportunity, to sheer off into scientific or theological observation.

Shyness or indifference? Impossible now to say.

A particularly virulent strain of smallpox destroyed Lady Talgarth's beauty when she was twenty-three. From then on she wore the veil, and as far as we know the two never met again.

There has never been any proof that Topcliffe fathered the child of his housekeeper, Mary Tratton, but she was unusually well-provided for in his will, as was the boy.

12

Mary's boy grows strong.
Each day his eyes
allow a little more of wonder to intrude
so his mind might
discover apt descriptions.

I rode him to the sea.
He thought the boats had
dropped out of the sky.
Last night he heard the breeze
blur into the elms
and asked me if it was
moonlight whispering.

13

Alexander Topcliffe to Lady Talgarth

My Dear Lady,

Let us say, I find the moon unutterably beautiful, not despite but because of its craters and shadows. When Galileo gazed upon its surface, Aristotle died. And the new world, our world, was born.

That no man has landed there, nor ever shall, gives that beauty an increase all its own.

Some remain condemned only to the mind's fecundity.

P.S. Do you still keep a crow's feather on your pillow to ward away black dreams?

14

I dream sometimes the sea has hammered so hard at the darkness the whole land shifts under the waves. The house drowns. My papers fall like snowflakes on the flood. The furniture is scattered driftwood and the house settles on the sea's floor, eels coiled into its chimneys. Then a sunset red as a wound illuminates the quelled country. A sliver of moon inaugurates its kingdom, and I wake without peace.

15

We refer to Topcliffe casually as a scientist but he did not refer to himself as one and nor could he have done, for the term was not then even invented, being coined by the philosopher Whewell in the nineteenth century.

Yet for Topcliffe, despite his membership of the Royal Society, this was not the only world. World upon world overlapped us here. What we see in the visible, he writes in his diary, is but one manifestation of manifold reality. The world of our senses is a little epiphany, a showing-forth under the singular order of signs appropriate to us. All creatures have their languages assigned.

16

Light arrives
from far resorts.

How beautiful the boy's face
beaming like a little moon
over the planet he circles.

It cannot be long.

A great weakening.
The blood's normal functions
are fouling, the spleen enlarged.
Anaemia, a great fatigue.
I sense the organs slowing
as they falter.
Gums weep blood, the bowels dreary.

Everything runs down except
the pain: thus is the balance of this
trim machine exalted,
consciousness rising
as the void dilates.

17

The camera creeps about his study.
Sheets decorated with equations
scatter the desk.
A microscope catches a flick of sunlight.
Hooke's *Micrographia* lies open
at an illustration of the underside
leaf of a stinging nettle
junctioning with hypodermic points.
On the wall a chart roughly-printed:
Harvey's experiments on
valve-action in the veins.
On an inlaid table by the window
the five regular polyhedra sit and glisten.
The camera glides over them
out through the window
and for a five-second take
butterflies its way across the garden.

18

Giordano Bruno posited
no point of fixity
for if the universe is infinite
what criterion could fixity obtain?
Certainly not the sun
although the sun gives heat
more than enough in fact to burn
your man in the first year
of this inquiring century.

Or was it the last year
of the century before?

19

Lady Amanda Talgarth to Alexander Topcliffe

I have heard from those who were once your friends in London that you are ill and word is out that you are very ill indeed.

How I long to see you. Yet such a visit might afflict you with more grief than comfort.

What can I say? Except that if it is true, as you once assured me, that this is merely one aspect of one world and that in striding through the exit which we call our deaths we simply enter another and a larger life, then in that life, Sir, with my beauty restored, I might appreciate an earlier proposal.

20

. . . and to Mary Tratton the sum outright of seven hundred pounds for the maintenance of herself and her son. Also that provision be made for their accommodation in this house for the duration of their lives. Also that the boy be ensured access at all times during his education to my library and scientific instruments . . .

21

A suspicion I cannot prove: that the blood too is constituted out of complementarities, that it is not homogeneous. And that one element within it, sagged or sapped, might then provoke the other into venom. This seems the pattern of all systems of life.

So a war like the bloody and terrible one that ripped this land may be going on inside my veins.

If I had a lens a thousand times stronger than my microscope affords, would I then see them battling? Their shapes? And understanding the conflict with such graphic evidence, might I then assist in restoring the balance?

Can men with their eyes to lenses help restore peace to the world's bodies?

22

Alexander Topcliffe died of what we would call leukemia compounded with sickle-cell anaemia. The guesses he made at what was going on in his body must now strike us as very shrewd. Lacking the diagnostic technique with which he might have identified his own disease, still his diaries show us the rudiments of the scientific method which lets us name and describe that disease today.

After his death Mary Tratton continued to live at Ingleton Hall with her son who was educated to a high standard, according to the strict stipulation of Topcliffe's will. The boy later went on to become a scientist of some small repute.

Lady Amanda Talgarth never married and lived in retirement until her death at 87.

23

The camera, starting out from Ingleton
heads down hills towards the sea
makes a jackdaw circuit round the harbour
(soundtrack-winds wince in the rigging)
looks out across the swell and catches
one far sail, turns back
through the Abbey ruins
then speeded-up returns
to the bottom of the little field
by Ingleton and fixes focus
zooming on his tombstone.

Now the lens reads carefully,
as though a finger underlined
the lichened inscription:

Alexander Topcliffe

An Enquirer

1620-1668

5

Hearts to keep this Law

To Anthony Rudolf

Hearts to keep this Law

> 'Or who should tend
> the sores of lazars?
> (For anthropos is not always kind.)'
> David Jones

Observe the Law: you have no option. Chronicle
Its blessings and its misdemeanours
From those who set teeth sharp as blades
Against it; to those who throw a lifetime's
Arms around its neck, faithful as swans.

Trace its lineaments in stone, in flesh, in smoke.
Number its pilgrims, the quirky swarms
And cold migrations of your brothers.

Hear it clamour up against the wall
As men with oscillating heads and hearts
Cry out to the Lord of Israel
To pay attention to His wounded children.
And listen to the silence where it disappeared
Into the holes
That crater Europe.

Place your ears beneath a stranger's
Clothes in the drawer. Wrap
The latest headlines in used bandages.
Throw the switches on your self-possessed
Machines, little household gods that cry out
Litanies of information and lament.

Dip sharpened steel in black ink, write
A line of zeroes, extinguished cries

Mouths forever open to their silences.
A single star in the sky
Closes its eye.

⁂

In the Billy Rose Garden in Jerusalem
Zadkine's Orpheus is riddled
With poetry that rises through his own
Bronze skin; a lyre shafts his torso—
He is sheer song,
World incised with a world's beseeching
This alchemist of breath
Who fluted hell
Fingers astray in the strings' blessing.

His body demolished mostly
Leaving his song the scaffold.

⁂

Take Kafka's eyes.

They stare right through emaciated furniture
In the insurance building. Outside
A corridor continues coughing.

These eyes startle when the tongue
Speaks Yiddish, the ear hears Czech
Or bony fingers drive a nib through German.

Two rose windows
Ready to melt in the sun.
This dry pair once soaked up the flood
When one extra tear
Would have scuttled the ark.

(He was he said
A parable the Law discarded)

How they scrutinise the fairy tale he writes:
A frontier appears, farmhouses
Tremble as lorries throttle by.
A soldier laughs. An old woman
Stands startled by her clothes line.

Vague in early mist you make out
Rudiments of a barbed-wire fence.
Interned behind it blazing are those eyes.

*

In Leonardo's drawing of the foetus in the womb
The figure crouches in a nut that's been
Split open by the artist's inquisition.

The kindness of the page will close
Its gourd and re-connect
Its blood supply.

And when in 1674
John Dwight fashioned his dead daughter Lydia
In the stoneware of the Fulham Factory

Clutching the cut flower of her days
Her little features properly express
How each of us should be entitled
With a stone, however small
To number the departures.

Under the law she must at least be named.

*

If the Law is engraved on your heart
Then your heart is a stone
If the Law fills your eyes, eclipsing the light
Pluck them out—they are gazing on idols
If you have stitched the Law into your clothes
Beware the moth

(For it is wind, is shadow
the echo of the sun underwater
it travels swifter than
your fingers or your tongue)

Though the Law is ready
Always to bestow its leather heart
Cooked in the ovens
Of various dispensations
Between the Mediterranean
And the Baltic coast
Still the Law is symmetry:
No man can balance its tightrope.
Any dawn without warning
It could divorce you

Take you aside with a yawn and say,
I have swallowed your words
I've slept in the smell of your hair
I have let you scratch me where there was no itch
And where in any case
I never dreamt of comfort.
My friend, it's time we parted company:
I'm late already. As for yourself
You have an appointment with a different fire.
This time your own heart and its particulars
  are specified.

So
Don't overcook it.
Don't season it with too much
Sweetness and discretion.
Don't insist you left it on a train
As the engine's smoke unwrote
The language of the sky.

Remember our children.
In every one of their
Uncounted and unshed tears
A rainbow.

After Purgatorio Canto XVI

Infringement of hell and night divested
  of planets through a bankrupt sky
  (like an orrery seized-up and rusted)
never clamped such a visor over my eye
  as that coarse spew of incinerator smoke
  making the little world in the eyelid die
and close itself to heaven for suffering's sake;
  faithful in his wisdom my companion steered
  himself to lean on, out of my shadow's wake.
As a blind man shuffles after his guide
  so as not to reel back in terror
  from the map creasing in his closed head
I stumbled through sharp and salted air
  listening to my leader who repeated
  "Of all things, don't get separated from me here."
I heard voices, each one attempting to say
  a prayer for peace and the Lord's mercy
  to the Lamb of God who carries sins away.
Agnus Dei, they began in harmony
  linked in measure and degree
  so that one order comprehended many.
"Are these then spirits, Master, I am hearing?"
  And he: "Yes. As their sins are loosed
  the knot of their anger is disappearing."
Then: "Who are you, sojourning where no sun
  casts noon, measuring shadows and disinterring
  the lost race of time we have outrun?"
Thus that voice, then my Master's followed:
  "Answer him. Then ask if the route to heaven
  starts up from here." So I: "O fellow
creature, pounding yourself so the leaven
  bread of your soul should warm and rise,

  companion me. Share a marvel I've been given."
"I'll follow in faith" this fellow replies
 "as far as my steps have been allowed
 and if this smoke occlude our eyes
let words clarify what furnaces cloud."
 And so I began: "It is death
 itself permits the shedding of this shroud
to let me rise from Hell's scorched breath
 to stand before you here; and God's grace
 permits this vision of outmoded truth.
So do not hide from me the face
 and name you journeyed with on earth.
 Tell us the way: your words will help us pass."
"The name I had was Mark Lombard.
 I loved the world's long-gone perfection. To rise
 continue straight along—and pray for me to God."
And I replied: "You have my promise
 but I'm troubled by something you said.
 The world indeed is void of all perfection
where the wicked weep only at the sight of good.
 Tell me the source of this murderous infection."
 A trick of grief caught in his throat
then he began: "Brother, the world's defection
 from the will of God has blinded you and it
 for you with fire still in your veins
refer all causes up to where the saints have sat
 as if each movement linked back there by metal chains.
 If that were so, your choice would be a lie
good and evil as beyond our will as are the seasons.
 True judgement's given from the brightness in the sky
 and shone with compassed purpose, kills the dark
but this illumination is not enforced on high

therefore the good and bad about you are man's work.
From His hand comes but a simple soul
finding delight for celebration's sake
  but trifles for their own sake soon beguile
  and the Law rears up a tower of restraint
to keep small benefits in proper scale
  so stop them cloying into evil. When the very fount
  of truth on earth's polluted, what should the children
drink, whose father sucks at the greasy font?
  However loud unholy loves sing in the cauldron
  no demerit in our nature put them there
but wicked guidance. Two suns once smiled on
  Rome, dividing empire business from the world of prayer.
  Now one sun's swallowed up the other
and blinds with dazzle where before the pair
  lit up a world enslaved by neither.
  If you're still sceptical, observe the ear
of corn (since it's from seeds we later gather).
  On the land veined by Adige and Po
  valour and courtesy walked once hand in hand together
where today only the lowest of the low
  would creep across it, shuffling, veiled.
  There are only three old men still living now
by whom those lost commandments are fulfilled,
  in whom the ancient days rebuke the new:
  good Gherardo, Currado da Palazzo
and Guido da Castel (may they all
  be gathered into the Lord's own courtesy)
  while Rome's great church again must fall
in filth, installing Empire in the Holy See."
  "Ah Mark" I said "you argue well
  and I can see now why the sons of Levi

were debarred from wealth, in service to the tabernacle
  but who's this Gherardo, glittering like a last *trouvaille*
  a reproach from time's grey hairs to our brute laughter?"
"Now it is time for me to leave. I
  only know Gherardo from his name and daughter
  Gaia. See the smoke brighten like a dawn sky
with the angel's glory. I shall be seen by him hereafter
  but not now. God bless you. I must go."
  So he turned and said nothing as his steps grew softer.

Coda

Shroud

1 The Relic

It was the belief of the Docetists of Tyre that God had not suffered in the person of the Saviour, and that the passion on the cross had been by way of a display to beguile would-be believers. God could not suffer because God is, *ipso facto*, perfect, and suffering is a form of imperfection. Pain is a voice with which the human spirit calls out from inside its own incompletion. To ascribe such an incompleteness to the Almighty would be to impugn the divine *pleroma*, and thereby perpetrate a philosophical imbecility.

It was for this reason that their greatest relic was the White Shroud, which carried no stains of blood, sweat or tears. No face besmirched its surface. No ribs were numbered like Gothic cross-beams, nor were there five sacred marks, for there were none at all. This unstained shroud, preserved by Joseph of Arimathea after the so-called resurrection, was the one token of proof the Docetists needed: God suffered nothing on the day entitled by the heretics Good Friday.

2 THE TEXT

The cotton sheet of the White Shroud might be empty but the mind, even of a Docetist, is not. So soon there grew around the relic a textual tradition. This tradition would in time include the insistence of Scotus Erigena (no Docetist he, though suspected of heterodoxy) that the most appropriate name for God is *Nihilum*, uncontaminated as he is with any form of *Quidditas*. One cannot speak of what He is because there is no 'whatness' in Him. Had they not been separated by chronology, faith and prohibition, the Docetists might even have quoted the final words of Rav Shneur Zalma of Lyady in 1813: 'All I can see is the holy nothingness which gives life to the world.'

3 The Commentary

All holy texts require a commentary, for otherwise the human tongue would have no function except to clack. So the original Docetist text, a commentary really on the blankness of the White Shroud and the unutterable silence of God, generated in its turn a commentary which proliferated with every passing century.

The relic was displayed on a wall in the Docetist cathedral in Tyre (the north wall, for reasons now lost to exegesis). But by the seventh century the commentaries surrounding the shroud outspanned the original dimensions of the cotton sheet itself, many times over.

Commentaries continued to be written, of course, it being in the nature of a commentary never to be satisfactorily concluded. The north wall was now full. A meeting was held and a young Docetist scholar made a suggestion which astonished the ancient disciples. Since the shroud was blank, he said, and since both text and commentary were no more than a guide to that eloquent mute whiteness, why not simply place all the words of text and explication upon the cotton of the shroud, thereby combining the origin of the tradition with its subsequent elaboration, and eliding any distinction between space and truth on the north wall?

4 The Church

In the cathedral of the Docetists in Tyre, there hangs an enormous text upon the north wall. It is printed on cloth. Hundreds upon hundreds of individual commentaries speak of the White Shroud which once enfolded the body of Jesus. The body, in its empirical impersonation of death, had left no lasting mark upon its relic, because it was in truth the body of God, which speaks in every instant the perfect nothingness of itself, without leaving any mark or substantial sign for the credulous to venerate.

Although tradition holds that the shroud has long ago disintegrated and fallen into the earth, the words of the monument remain to this day. They speak of a stainless winding sheet and sudarium, something free entirely from any trace of history or pain, like the tiny white spaces we can sometimes still make out between the sacred words of our tradition.

www.ingramcontent.com/pod-product-compliance
Lightning Source LLC
Chambersburg PA
CBHW031156160426
43193CB00008B/384